THE BRAINIAC'S BOOK OF

ROBOTS AND AI

Greetings young brainiac!
My name is ROB3RTA and I'm going to
introduce you to a few of my robot friends.
Some of them might look different than you
expected—and they aren't all as chatty as me,
but they are all really good at their jobs.

THE BRAINIAC'S BOOK of
ROBOTS AND AI

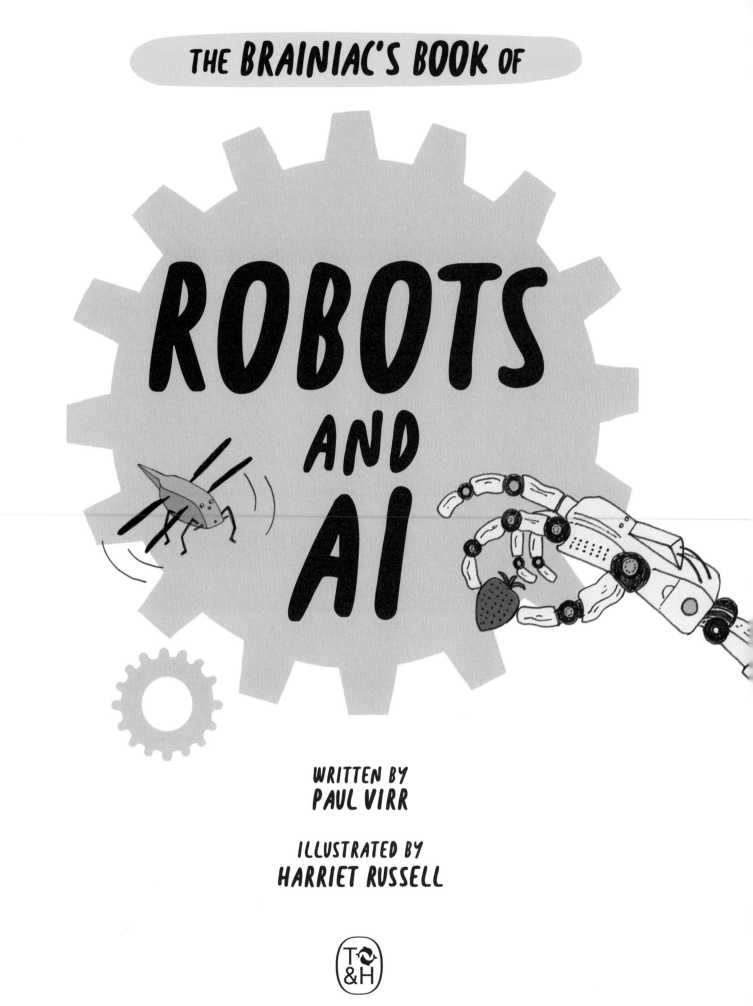

WRITTEN BY
PAUL VIRR

ILLUSTRATED BY
HARRIET RUSSELL

T&H

WHAT'S INSIDE?

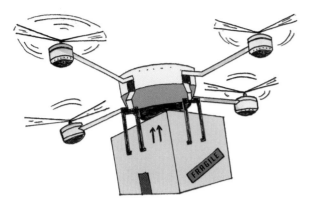

ROBOTS: FACT OR FANTASY?

EVERYONE KNOWS WHAT A ROBOT IS . . .

Robots are walking, talking, mechanical marvels, like the ones in sci-fi movies where they take over the world, right?

UNBEATABLE!
UNBREAKABLE!
UNBELIEVABLE!
ROBOTS

THEY SHOOT LASER BEAMS FROM THEIR EYES.

THEY ARE SUPER-SMART, WITH COMPUTER BRAINS IN THEIR METAL HEADS.

THEY HAVE INDESTRUCTIBLE METAL BODIES.

ROBOTS CAN RUN, FIGHT, FLY, AND TRANSFORM INTO DIFFERENT SHAPES.

THEY CAN THINK, SPEAK, AND UNDERSTAND HUMANS.

THEY ARE MEGA-STRONG, WITH MECHANICAL ARMS AND LEGS.

Robots with human-shaped bodies are called "humanoids." They appear in lots of futuristic movies, but most robots don't look like people at all.

REAL-LIFE ROBOTS

Robots are real, but don't panic—they aren't going to zap you with a laser!
Most robots are designed to do one useful job really well.
A movie about a real robot might not be all that exciting . . .

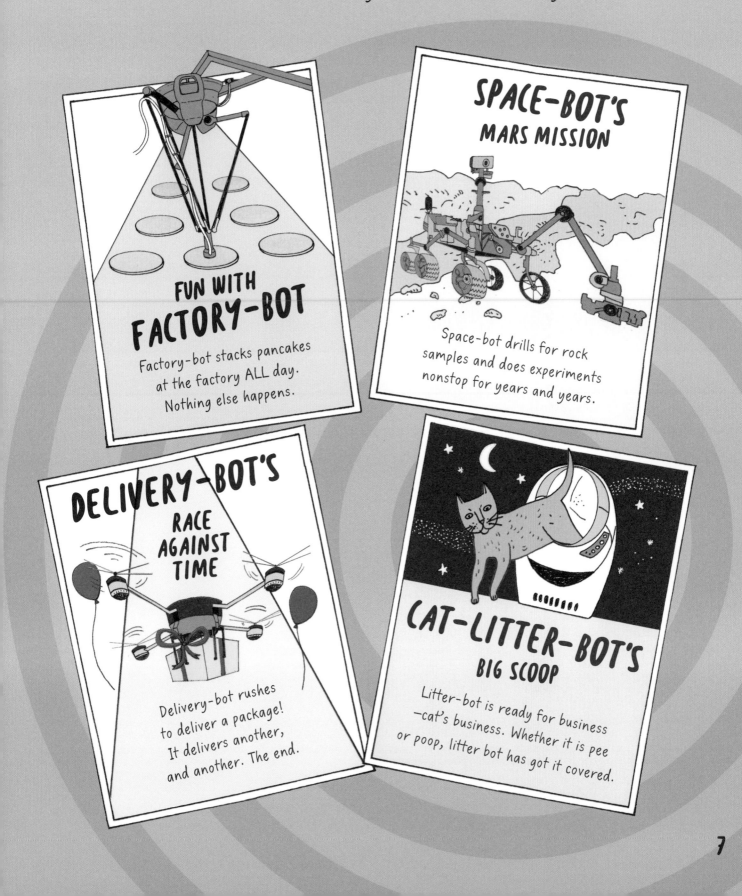

FUN WITH FACTORY-BOT

Factory-bot stacks pancakes at the factory ALL day. Nothing else happens.

SPACE-BOT'S MARS MISSION

Space-bot drills for rock samples and does experiments nonstop for years and years.

DELIVERY-BOT'S RACE AGAINST TIME

Delivery-bot rushes to deliver a package! It delivers another, and another. The end.

CAT-LITTER-BOT'S BIG SCOOP

Litter-bot is ready for business —cat's business. Whether it is pee or poop, litter bot has got it covered.

SO, WHAT IS A ROBOT?

Not sure? You're not alone—even robot experts are still puzzling this out!

NEED-TO-KNOW FACTS

The differences between machines, computers, and robots are not always clear. Here are the main characteristics of a robot:

FOOD-PACKING ROBOT

1. Robots **WORK.** They are machines that do jobs that are too dangerous, dirty, or dull for humans to do.

SPRAY-PAINTING ROBOT

2. Robots can **MOVE.** Some are fixed in place with moving parts, while others move around.

3. Robots **SENSE** the world around them and react to it.

ROBOT VACUUM CLEANER

4. Robots are **AUTOMATIC.** They usually do their jobs with little or no human help.

DRIVERLESS CAR

5. Robots can **DECIDE.** They are programmed by humans, but they can plan and make some decisions for themselves.

WHY WAS THE ROBOT DOG SCRATCHING?

IT HAD ROBOT-TICKS

STRANGE BUT TRUE!

The word "robot" was first used by Czech playwright Karel Ĉapek. In his sci-fi play *R.U.R.*, artificial workers do hard and boring jobs for humans. **"ROBOTA"** is the Czech word for "forced labor."

Scientists are working on an **ECO-BOT** that gets its power by grazing on dead flies, rotting plant matter, and even human poop!

Does reading this book make you feel sweaty, anxious, or dizzy? Then you could suffer from **ROBOPHOBIA**—an irrational fear of everything robotic.

The first Robot Olympics was held in Glasgow, Scotland in 1990. Sixty-eight robots from twelve countries competed in events such as wall climbing, pole balancing, and javelin throwing!

SPOT THE BOT!

It's time to turn robo-detective. Can you tell the **BOTS** from the **NOT-BOTS** in this lineup of mechanical suspects? Use the checklist below to help you.

ROBOT SPOTTER CHECKLIST

A. IS IT A MACHINE?
B. DO YOU PROGRAM IT TO DO JOBS?
C. DOES IT MOVE?
D. CAN IT SENSE THE WORLD AROUND IT?
E. CAN IT MAKE DECISIONS FOR ITSELF?
F. IS IT AUTOMATIC?

Generally speaking, the more check marks on the checklist, the closer the machine is to a robot.
Turn to p. 62 for the answers.

1
VENDING MACHINE
It's a machine and has moving parts, but is it a robot?

5
AUTOMATED LAWN MOWER
It does a job that humans don't want to do, like most robots.

6
SELF-DRIVING CAR
Is this in fact an undercover robot?

7
RADIO-CONTROLLED BOAT
It moves, but a human steers it around, so who's making the decisions?

Robots aren't always easy to spot. Some everyday gadgets have a little bit of "robotness" in their abilities. Of course, I'm 100% genuine robot.

2
PARKING LOT BARRIER
This barrier detects when a car approaches, and raises itself.

3
WASHING MACHINE
It can wash your socks, but is it a robot in disguise?

4
DRONE COPTER
It moves, but can it make decisions?

8
COMPUTER
It can be programmed to do different jobs, but is it a robot?

9
SMART SPEAKER
It understands commands and answers questions, but it doesn't move. Hmm . . .

10
HEALTHCARE HELPER
It passes the test for having a useful job and moving around. What do you think?

THE FIRST ROBOTS

Robots were around 2,000 years ago—before electricity was even discovered!

AUTOMATA: THE ANCIENT ROBOTS THAT AMAZED THE WORLD

Automata were machines that seemed to move and have a life of their own. Powered by falling weights, water, steam, pendulums, and later by clockwork springs, they often imitated people or animals.

Over 1,900 years ago, long before self-driving cars, engineer and math wiz Heron of Alexandria invented a programmable **SELF-DRIVING CART**, powered by a falling weight.

About 800 years ago, medieval inventor Al-Jazari designed an ingenius **ROBOTIC ELEPHANT CLOCK**. Every half hour, a bird spun around, a serpent moved, and the elephant driver struck a cymbal.

BONG!
BONG!

All-around genius Leonardo da Vinci designed a **ROBOT KNIGHT** more than 500 years ago. Workings hidden inside the armor enabled it to move and even raise its visor.

SPLAT!

In the 1730s, inventor Jacques de Vaucanson built some incredible automata, including a figure that played the tambourine and a robotic **DIGESTING DUCK**. It could flap its wings, appear to eat grain, and poop!

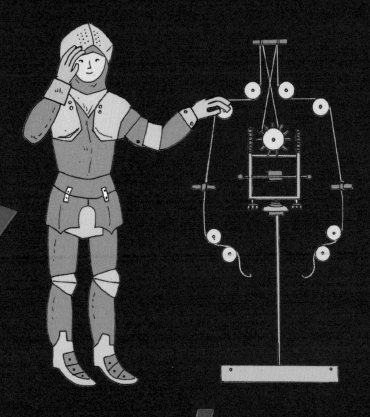

WHIRR

Clockmaker Juanelo Turriano built an automaton of a mechanical **PRAYING MONK** for the King of Spain over 450 years ago. It could roll along and move its arms.

In the 1700s, watchmaker Pierre Jaquet-Droz and his sons Henri-Louis and Jean-Frédéric Leschot built awesome humanlike automata. **THE WRITER** is a mechanical boy that writes with a quill pen and real ink.

ROBOT WORKSHOP

HOW TO MAKE A ROBOT MOVE WITH SIMPLE MECHANICS!

BRAINIAC HACK: CAM MECHANISM

Automata move in a lifelike way using rotating discs, or **CAMS**. As a cam turns it makes a lever, or **FOLLOWER**, rise and fall.

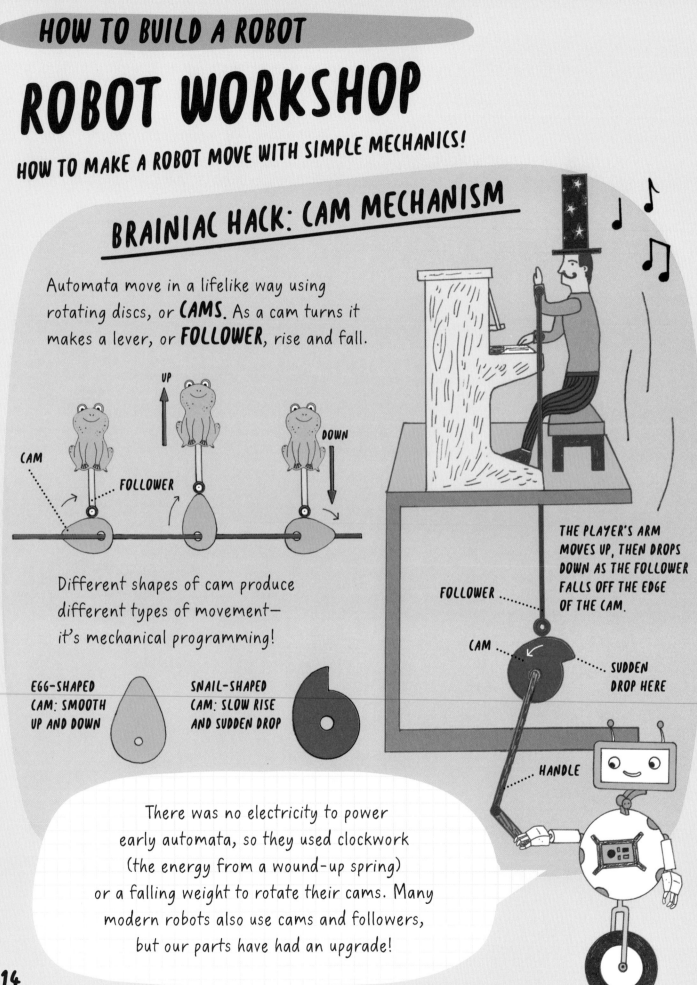

UP

DOWN

CAM

FOLLOWER

Different shapes of cam produce different types of movement—it's mechanical programming!

EGG-SHAPED CAM: SMOOTH UP AND DOWN

SNAIL-SHAPED CAM: SLOW RISE AND SUDDEN DROP

THE PLAYER'S ARM MOVES UP, THEN DROPS DOWN AS THE FOLLOWER FALLS OFF THE EDGE OF THE CAM.

FOLLOWER

CAM

SUDDEN DROP HERE

HANDLE

There was no electricity to power early automata, so they used clockwork (the energy from a wound-up spring) or a falling weight to rotate their cams. Many modern robots also use cams and followers, but our parts have had an upgrade!

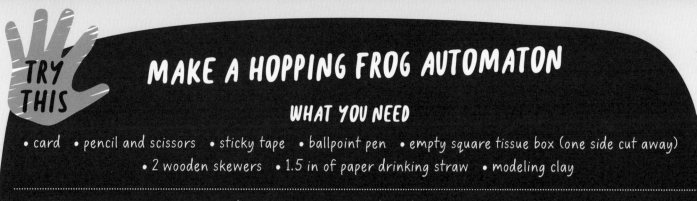
MAKE A HOPPING FROG AUTOMATON

WHAT YOU NEED

• card • pencil and scissors • sticky tape • ballpoint pen • empty square tissue box (one side cut away)
• 2 wooden skewers • 1.5 in of paper drinking straw • modeling clay

1. Draw the frog, cam, and follower onto card and cut them out.
Fold and stick down the follower as shown.

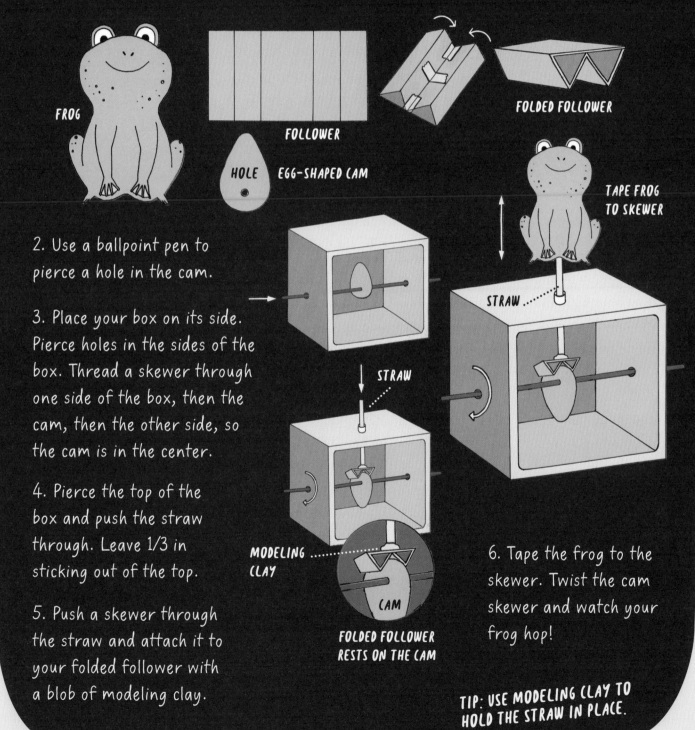

FROG

FOLLOWER

FOLDED FOLLOWER

HOLE   EGG-SHAPED CAM

TAPE FROG
TO SKEWER

2. Use a ballpoint pen to pierce a hole in the cam.

STRAW

3. Place your box on its side. Pierce holes in the sides of the box. Thread a skewer through one side of the box, then the cam, then the other side, so the cam is in the center.

STRAW

4. Pierce the top of the box and push the straw through. Leave 1/3 in sticking out of the top.

MODELING
CLAY

CAM

5. Push a skewer through the straw and attach it to your folded follower with a blob of modeling clay.

FOLDED FOLLOWER
RESTS ON THE CAM

6. Tape the frog to the skewer. Twist the cam skewer and watch your frog hop!

TIP: USE MODELING CLAY TO
HOLD THE STRAW IN PLACE.

15

MECHANICAL MOVERS

Modern robots use wheels, rotors, robot limbs, or thrusters to move, driven by devices called **ACTUATORS**. Check out the body parts that help modern robots get a move on!

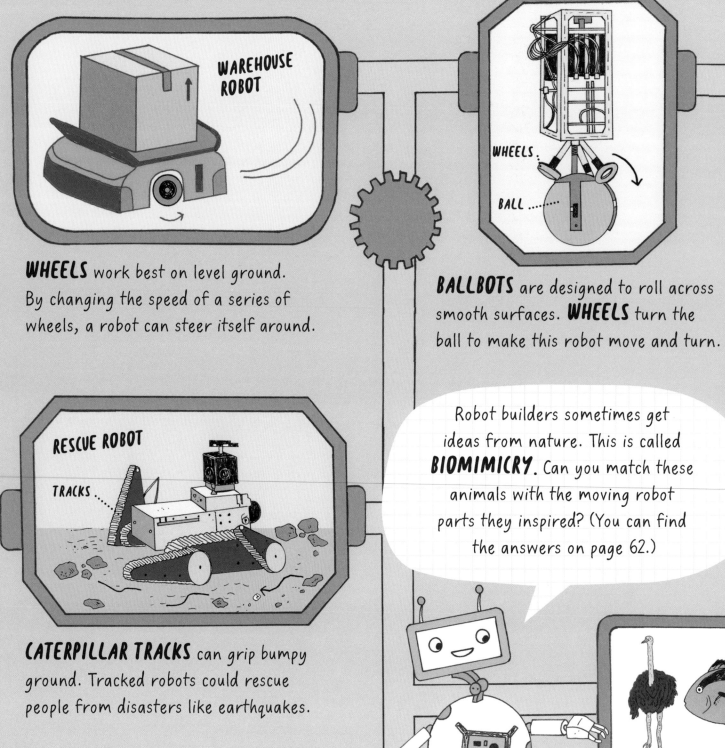

WAREHOUSE ROBOT

WHEELS

BALL

WHEELS work best on level ground. By changing the speed of a series of wheels, a robot can steer itself around.

BALLBOTS are designed to roll across smooth surfaces. **WHEELS** turn the ball to make this robot move and turn.

RESCUE ROBOT

TRACKS

CATERPILLAR TRACKS can grip bumpy ground. Tracked robots could rescue people from disasters like earthquakes.

Robot builders sometimes get ideas from nature. This is called **BIOMIMICRY.** Can you match these animals with the moving robot parts they inspired? (You can find the answers on page 62.)

TWO-LEGGED robots are being designed with mechanical muscles to move their legs. Balancing is tricky!

MANY LEGS make it easier for robots to balance. This hexapod robot scuttles along on six legs like a bug.

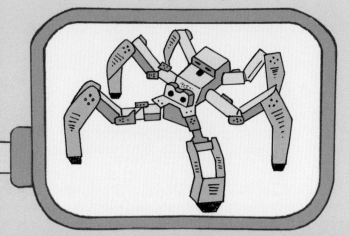

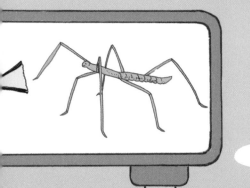

UNDERCOVER WILDLIFE SPY

FIN

TAIL

FINS and a swishing tail move robotic fish through the water.

DEEP-SEA EXPLORER

PROPELLER

PROPELLERS are found on underwater robots like submarines. In the sky, propeller-powered drones might soon be making deliveries.

THRUSTERS are used on satellites and space probes to carry out missions in space.

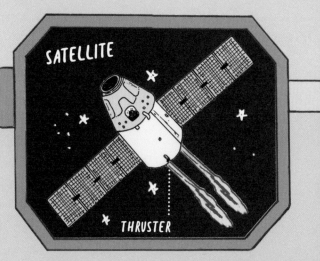

SATELLITE

THRUSTER

FLIP FORWARD >>> to pages 34-35 for more about **BIOMIMICRY**

HANDY ROBOTS

GET TO GRIPS WITH THE GRABBING PARTS THAT ROBOTS USE

BRAINIAC HACK: END EFFECTORS

Instead of hands like us, robots use **END EFFECTORS** to do their work. These parts can often be swapped to do different jobs, from grabbing and lifting to engineering work.

MECHANICAL ROBOT ARMS are used in factories to weld, cut, glue, and paint.

MAGNETIC GRIPPERS have electromagnets at the end of a robot arm. They pick up and move magnetic metals in factories.

VACUUM GRIPPERS use suction power to hold flat objects with a suction cup.

FINGER GRIPPERS are two- or three-fingered claws that mimic a human hand. They can work with tools and objects that humans use.

BUILD A ROBOT HAND

WHAT YOU NEED

• pencil   • card   • scissors   • paper drinking straws   • sticky tape   • string

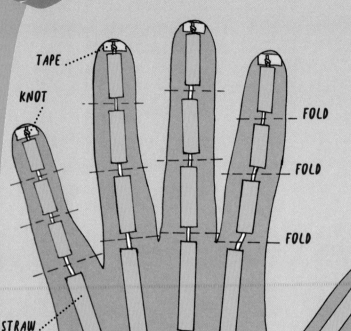

TAPE

KNOT

FOLD

FOLD

FOLD

STRAW

STRAW

FOLD

STRING

1. Draw around your hand and wrist onto card. Cut out the hand shape.

2. Make folds on each finger as shown.

3. Snip and tape three short pieces of straw along each finger between the folds you made. Tape one along the thumb.

4. Tape ten longer pieces of straw to the palm of the hand, as shown.

5. Thread string through the straws on each finger, through the straws on the hand, and out the other side. Knot and secure each piece of string with sticky tape at the fingertips.

6. Pull on the bottom ends of the string to close the fingers.

TRY PICKING UP SOMETHING LIGHT, LIKE A TOILET PAPER TUBE OR AN EMPTY DRINK CAN.

EXPLANATION:

Human hands have tendons that attach the arm muscles to the finger bones. They work like levers to close the fingers and grip objects. Instead of tendons, robot hands have cables, or in this case string!

HOW DO ROBOTS SENSE STUFF?

Unlike us, robots don't come with ready-made senses. To gather information about their surroundings, they have to be fitted with **SENSORS**. Humans have five main senses, but robots are only designed with the sensors they need.

HEARING

Robots use microphones to pick up sound signals.

MICROPHONE

WAAAH!

SIGHT

Cameras and light sensors help robots to "see." They also use lasers to map what's around them.

PHOTOCELL LIGHT SENSOR

DIGITAL CAMERA LIGHT SENSOR

BUMP!

SMELL & TASTE

Chemical detectors are the robot version of the senses of smell and taste.

TOUCH

All kinds of touch and pressure sensors let robots feel what they touch— or bump into! Pressure sensors allow robot hands to hold delicate objects.

TOUCH SENSOR

CARBON MONOXIDE DETECTOR

GUESS WHAT?
ROBOTS NEED GYRO SENSORS, TILT DETECTORS, AND ACCELEROMETERS TO TELL THEM IF THEY ARE MOVING OR STILL.

> Some sensors mimic human senses, but others give robots almost superhuman powers, like X-ray vision!

SUPER SENSES

INFRARED CAMERAS let robots "see" heat. They can detect a living thing in complete darkness!

BEEEEP!

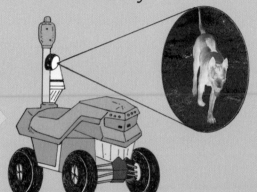

Robots use **GAS DETECTORS** to sense dangerous leaks that humans can't smell.

THERMAL IMAGING CAMERA

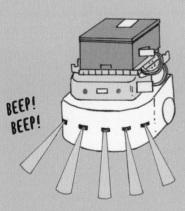

BEEP! BEEP!

BIOMETRIC SENSORS take scientific measurements. Medical robots can check whether patients have a fever. Cool!

PROXIMITY SENSORS let robots know when something is near, even if they don't actually touch it.

WHY MAKE ROBOTS THAT CAN SEE, HEAR, AND SMELL?

IT'S COMMON SENSORS!

ARE BOTS BRAINY OR NOT?

How do robots know what to do? Do they have **BRAINS** that think, like us?

A robot's moving parts and sensors are connected to a small, onboard **COMPUTER** called a **MICROCONTROLLER**. It's the closest thing a robot gets to a **BRAIN!**

MICROCONTROLLER

COMPUTER PROGRAMMER

COMPUTER CODE

Computers can't actually think— they follow the instructions they are **PROGRAMMED** with.

PROGRAMMERS write step-by-step instructions in **CODE**—a language that computers understand.

Some robots can solve problems, react to sensors and make decisions, but their microcontrollers can't **THINK** like a human brain. My friend here can ONLY pick out broken cookies, but humans can decide which ones to eat!

REJECTED!

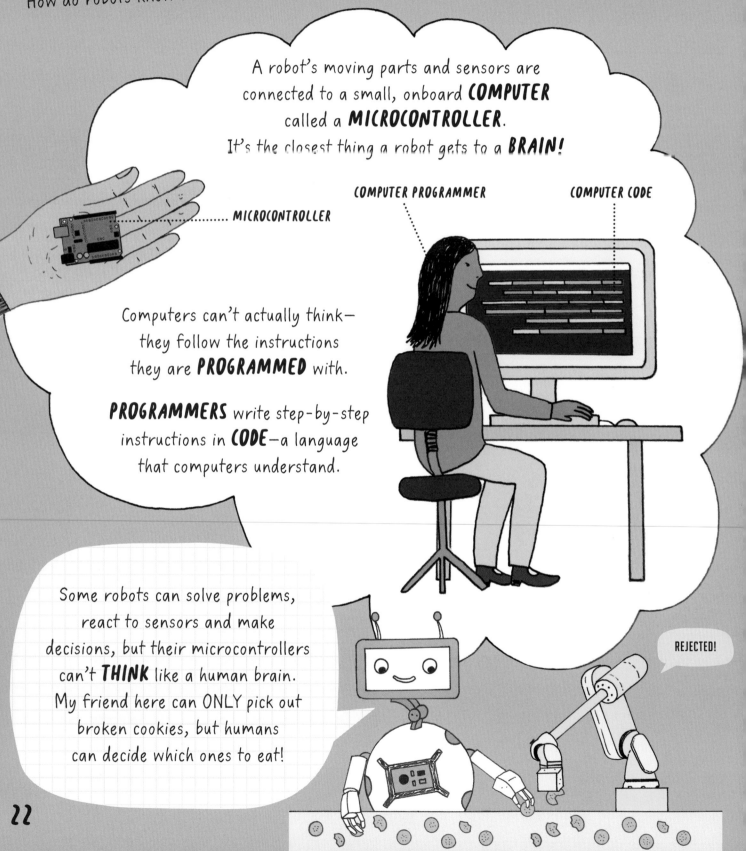

BRAINBOXES GO HEAD TO HEAD

Take a look at how human and robot smarts compare . . .

HUMAN

We humans decide what to do based on our own goals. Or based on what we have to do!

We can remember information and learn new skills.

We can usually work stuff out, even if we don't have all the information.

SLURP!

ROBOT

Robots can only perform tasks that have been programmed by a human.

Some robots are programmed to learn, but only in a limited way—and they don't always get it right!

CAT!

Robots may act smart, but they are only as clever as the human that programmed them.

BEEEEEEEP!

NO SWIMMING

WHY DID THE BRAIN GO RUNNING?

IT WANTED TO JOG ITS MEMORY!

DATA DUMP — MECHANICAL MINDS

Travel back in time to meet some of the super-brains behind the first computers.

NUMBER CRUNCHERS, CODE CRACKERS, AND A LANGUAGE IN 1s AND 0s

In 1679, math wiz Gottfried Leibniz developed the **BINARY** system—a number system made up of **1**s and **0**s. Today, binary is the code used in all computers!

> MY TWO FAVORITE NUMBERS ARE 1 AND 0.

GUESS WHAT?
THE DATE 1679 WRITTEN IN BINARY LOOKS LIKE THIS: 11010001111

GOTTFRIED LEIBNIZ

CHARLES BABBAGE

> MY COMPUTER WAS AN UNFINISHED MASTERPIECE. SNIFF!

Meet inventor Charles Babbage. In 1837 he designed the Analytical Engine. It was never built, but it would have been the world's first **PROGRAMMABLE COMPUTER.**

CAM

LOOK! CAMS—JUST LIKE AN AUTOMATON.

FLIP BACK <<< to page 14 to find out more about programming with CAMS

The mathematician Ada Lovelace helped Charles Babbage work out a way to program his computer using punched cards. It was the first **COMPUTER PROGRAM.**

GET WITH THE PROGRAM, PEOPLE!

The holes and "not holes" of a punched card can provide a mechanical way to program a computer with the **1**s and **0**s of binary.

ADA LOVELACE

THIS COMPUTER REALLY IS COLOSSAL!

Luckily, today's computer programmers don't have to punch holes in paper or write thousands of 1s and 0s. They write code that is then translated into binary code by another program.

Colossus, the enormous World War II codebreaking machine, was the world's first **DIGITAL ELECTRONIC COMPUTER.** Colossus was programmed with more than 1,500 electronic switches, called valves, and paper tape punched with holes.

HOW DO YOU PROGRAM A ROBOT?

Before offloading chores onto a robot, you need to tell it what to do, and how to do it!

BRAINIAC HACK: ALGORITHMS

An **ALGORITHM** is just a set of instructions that you follow to do a particular job—like baking a cake.

When you bake, you need to do each step in turn and **FOLLOW** the recipe **EXACTLY**.

ADD TWO EGGS. BEAT WELL AFTER EACH ADDITION.

If the instructions aren't **CORRECT**, then your cake will go wrong!

EXPLANATION:
So, an algorithm is a set of instructions that a robot's computer can use to help solve a problem or to make a decision about what to do.

BAKE FOR **ONE DAY** AT THE HOTTEST TEMPERATURE.

A programmed robot follows its instructions exactly, too. Get the instructions right and the robot will do what it is supposed to do.

MAZE ESCAPE

Write the instructions to tell the robot how to escape from the maze. Grab a pen and paper and draw the arrows in the correct order from the START to the FINISH.

PROGRAM INSTRUCTIONS

MOVE RIGHT ONE SPACE

MOVE UP ONE SPACE

MOVE LEFT ONE SPACE

MOVE DOWN ONE SPACE

Remember, the order is important.
Turn to page 62 for the answers!

START

FINISH

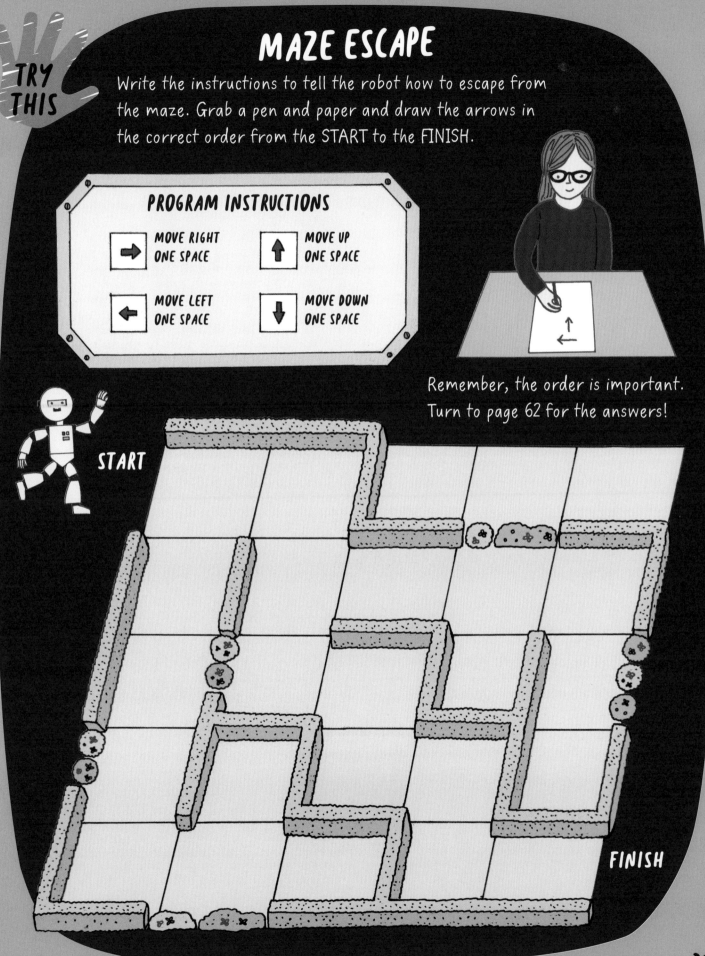

JOBS FOR ROBOTS

Most robots are made to do work, so what kinds of jobs do they do?

NEED-TO-KNOW FACTS

We humans are good at doing jobs that need different **SKILLS**, such as creativity, problem solving, and good communication.

THE NEW DESIGN IS READY!

But robots are perfect for jobs that are **DIRTY**, **DULL**, or **DANGEROUS**.

ROBOT JOB SKILLS

- **STRONGER AND FASTER THAN HUMAN WORKERS**
- **RARELY MAKE MISTAKES**
- **NEVER GET TIRED**
- **NEVER GET BORED**
- **DON'T GET HARMED DOING RISKY OR DIRTY JOBS**
- **NEVER TAKE A DAY OFF**

While humans are cozy in bed, robots work **NONSTOP**, making things in factories or lifting heavy loads in warehouses.

A robot **DOESN'T FEEL** hot or cold, it doesn't get sick, hungry, or thirsty, and it can work in complete darkness.

28

JUST THE JOB!

Robot arm Unimate went to work in a car factory in 1961 as the first industrial robot. It took over risky and repetitive jobs from human workers.

Sewer-cleaning robots are sent inside stinky sewer pipes. They blast away fatbergs, diapers, and other gross things that cause a blockage!

Remote-controlled cowherds work on ranches in the U.S. rounding up herds of headstrong cattle by waving flags on their robotic arms. Yee-haw!

MOOOO!

HOSPITAL HEROES

BUG-BUSTING, HARDWORKING ROBOTS ARE HERE TO HELP!

BRAINIAC HACK: MEDICAL ROBOTS

All kinds of robots are at work in hospitals right now, helping out doctors and nurses.

Computerized **CLEANING ROBOTS** are used to disinfect patients' rooms with ultraviolet (UV) light that kills germs. A robot is perfect for this job because UV rays are harmful to humans.

DOCTORS USE LIVE VIDEO TO CHAT WITH PATIENTS

ZAP! ZAP!

ZAP! ZAP!

ROBO DOG-TOR?

Medical robots allow doctors to visit patients with infectious diseases without putting themselves at risk.

Robots are not affected by germs and diseases that make humans sick. This makes them perfect for hospital work. They don't need to wear protective masks or clothing and are easy to clean at the end of the day!

ROBOTIC SURGERY

Surgeons use **ROBOTIC ARMS** to perform tricky operations.
As the surgeon moves their controls, the robot copies and
scales down the movement so it is tiny and super-accurate.

A SCREEN PROVIDES A ZOOMED-IN VIEW

ROBOT ARMS

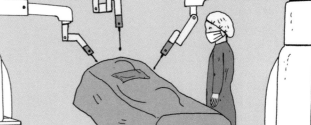

HAND
CONTROLS

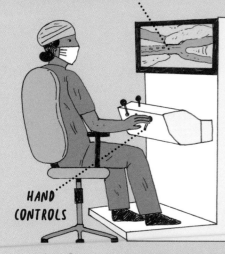

TRY THIS

TEST YOUR STEADY SKILLS!

Even with a robot's help, surgeons need to have incredibly steady hands.
Test your hand-eye coordination with these finicky challenges.

Use chopsticks to pick
up beads or marbles,
one at a time.

Use tweezers
to pick up grains
of rice and drop
them into an
empty bottle.

Use a knife and fork to cut
windows in a slice of bread.

THE INCREDIBOTS

WHEN THE GOING GETS TOUGH, BOTS KEEP GOING!

These superhero robots can tackle trouble in places where it's too **DANGEROUS** for human rescue crews to go.

HIGH-PRESSURE HOSE
BLASTS WATER

A **FIRE ROBOT** can roll into the heart of a blaze and battle the flames while the firefighters control it from a safe distance.

A BULLDOZER BLADE CLEARS OBSTACLES

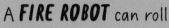

CAMERA

Different types of **RESCUE ROBOTS** can be sent to search for survivors following a natural disaster, like an earthquake. Robots can move around unstable ruins so rescue crews don't have to risk their lives.

ROBOT ARM TO MOVE DEBRIS

32

THERMAL
CAMERA

A **FLYING ROBOT** or "drone" can search a large area more quickly than rescuers on the ground. Its thermal camera can pick up the heat of a missing person and send live images back to the search team.

THERMAL
IMAGE

Dangerous situations need quick decisions, so rescue robots are worked by humans using **REMOTE CONTROL**. In the future, robots may be designed that can make decisions and explore by themselves.

ULTIMATE EXPLORERS

Robots can venture into places too **EXTREME** for humans to survive.

VOLCANO-BOT

1 FT

This small rolling robot made a 3D map while exploring deep inside a fiery volcano.

OCEAN ONE

Archeologists have used a **ROBOT DIVER** to recover pottery from an ancient shipwreck too deep for human divers to reach. The robot was controlled from a ship using an electrical cable.

GO WILD FOR ROBOTS

GOT A PROBLEM? A ROBOTIC ANIMAL COULD BE THE ANSWER!

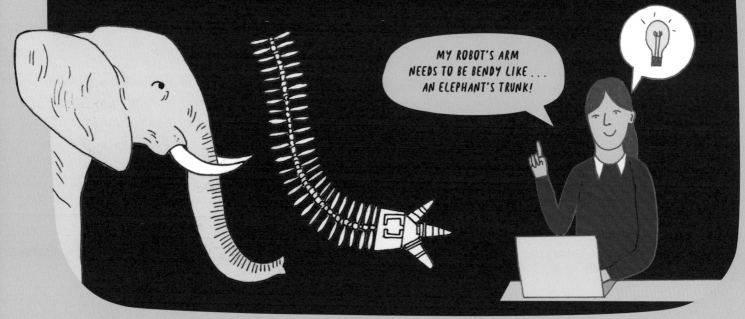

CREATURE FEATURES

Wild animals have changed slowly over millions of years to suit their different environments. When robot engineers want to solve a problem they sometimes take a shortcut by copying nature. This is called **BIOMIMICRY**.

MY ROBOT'S ARM NEEDS TO BE BENDY LIKE . . . AN ELEPHANT'S TRUNK!

BUZZ-BOTS

PROBLEM: pollution, habitat loss, and climate change have led to a drop in the number of bees. Farmers need bees to pollinate crops so that fruit and vegetables grow.

SOLUTION: build robotic bees to fly pollen from flower to flower.

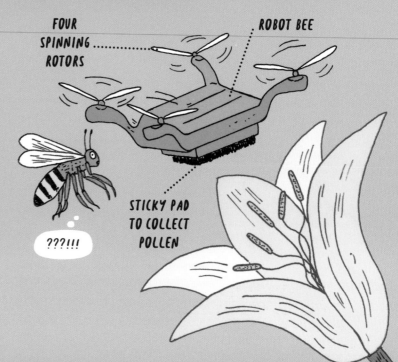

FOUR SPINNING ROTORS

ROBOT BEE

???!!!

STICKY PAD TO COLLECT POLLEN

CRAB-BOT

PROBLEM: rocky terrain and strong tides make exploring the seabed difficult.

SOLUTION: a crab's low, flat body and wide legs keep it from getting swept away, so create a giant crab-bot that can explore wrecks or clean up pollution.

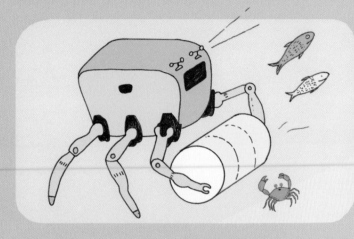

SNAKES ALIVE!

PROBLEM: most robots cannot get to hard-to-reach places.

SOLUTION: design a flexible snake-bot that can slither into cracks and over obstacles. It could repair pipes from the inside and could even investigate other planets!

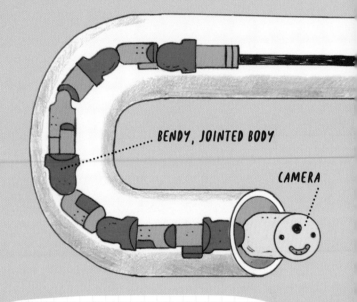

BENDY, JOINTED BODY

CAMERA

ROBO-BUDDY

PROBLEM: therapy dogs help patients feel calm and happy, but some people are afraid of dogs, or allergic. Also, dogs can spread germs between patients.

SOLUTION: create a waggy-tailed robo-dog that responds to being stroked, recognizes faces and voices—and can be wiped clean!

So far, no robot sensor can match a real dog's sense of smell. Trained sniffer dogs follow their noses to find anything from avalanche survivors to bombs.

DATA DUMP WATCH THIS SPACE

Space: there's no air to breathe, it can be boiling or freezing, and the travel takes forever.

CAN'T HANDLE SPACE? SEND A ROBOT IN YOUR PLACE!

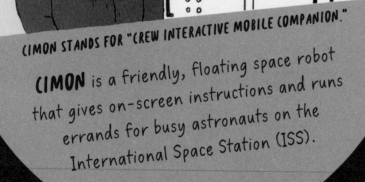

MY NAME IS CIMON, WHAT CAN I HELP YOU WITH?

CIMON STANDS FOR "CREW INTERACTIVE MOBILE COMPANION."

CIMON is a friendly, floating space robot that gives on-screen instructions and runs errands for busy astronauts on the International Space Station (ISS).

GUESS WHAT?
OVER 150 ROBOTS HAVE EXPLORED SPACE.

ISS

HUMAN-SHAPED ROBOTS
(called humanoids) have also spent time on the ISS. They don't need air or a protective spacesuit so they can do dangerous jobs as well as boring chores.

ROBONAUT 2 HAS SUCH NIMBLE FINGERS IT CAN OPERATE TOOLS AND FLIP FINICKY SWITCHES.

ROBONAUT 2

PERSEVERANCE MARS ROVER

PERSEVERANCE HAS TWENTY-THREE CAMERAS FOR TAKING PICTURES OF MARS—IT ALSO LIKES TAKING SELFIES!

Scientists on Earth can explore distant planets, such as Mars, by using a robot rover. Perseverance collects rock samples and stores them for future analysis.

Robotic **SPACE PROBES** travel vast distances to study the farthest reaches of the Solar System— and beyond.

VOYAGER 2

VOYAGER 2 HAS BEEN TRAVELING FOR OVER FORTY YEARS, TAKING PICTURES OF THE PLANETS IT PASSES.

There are two Voyager robots traveling through space. Both carry a special golden disc containing greetings from Earth just in case they are ever found by curious aliens!

Space scientists are developing robots to explore comets and asteroids. This **SPIKY SPACE EXPLORER** has eight points that will allow it to tumble across rugged space rocks.

HEDGEHOG

WHAT IS ARTIFICIAL INTELLIGENCE?

If robots aren't able to think like us, what about artificial intelligence?

NEED-TO-KNOW FACTS

HUMAN INTELLIGENCE isn't just about being brainy. Intelligence is:

- Learning and gaining skills
- Reasoning and solving problems
- Using memories to understand stuff
- Communication skills
- Learning from mistakes

And much more!

ARTIFICIAL INTELLIGENCE, or **AI**, is computer programming that can do at least one of the things on our human intelligence list. However, **GENERAL AI** that can do all of it hasn't been invented yet.

AI is all around us, from navigation apps to search engines. Some robots have **AI EXPERT SYSTEMS**, which can even diagnose illnesses. They seem intelligent because they store knowledge from real medical experts. (The AI can be quicker and more accurate!)

A-A-ACHOOOO!

YOU HAVE A COLD.

MEDICAL ROBOT

WHAT IS THE OPPOSITE OF ARTIFICIAL INTELLIGENCE?

REAL STUPID!

BRAIN-BOT TEST

In 1950, computer genius Alan Turing came up with a fun way to show whether a computer is capable of imitating a human. The **TURING TEST** is like a quiz with two hidden contestants—a person and a computer with AI.

HUMAN

COMPUTER WITH AI

350

400

ALAN TURING

Turing said that if you couldn't tell whose answers were whose, then the computer was showing intelligent behavior.

Some scientists are building a type of AI called **ARTIFICIAL NEURAL NETWORKS** to perform tricky tasks like face recognition. These are inspired by the way information gets passed between human brain cells. I think mine are working!

ROBOTS V. HUMANS

WE HAVE AI WINNER!

Can AI **BEAT** humans at their own **GAMES**? It looks like it can . . .

Around 250 years ago, a **MECHANICAL CHESS PLAYER** amazed audiences by beating some pretty good players. It appeared to be truly intelligent; however, it was a trick! A human player hid inside the chess table and worked levers to move the pieces.

I REALLY NEED TO GO TO THE BATHROOM!

I LOSE AGAIN!

In 1990, a computer program that plays **CHECKERS** became the first to compete in any human world championship. It came second, but by 2007 the makers of the program—called **CHINOOK**—had made it 100% unbeatable.

In 1997, an AI supercomputer called **DEEP BLUE** beat the world **CHESS CHAMPION**, Garry Kasparov. Deep Blue quickly worked out millions of possible moves before deciding what to do, then a human moved the pieces.

In 2011, **WATSON**, a computer programmed with AI, beat its human opponents to win a **TV QUIZ SHOW**. The AI could give accurate answers in less than three seconds.

WHERE DID IT ALL GO WRONG?!

I OWE IT ALL TO MY PROGRAMMER.

$1,000,000

GO is a more complicated game than chess, with more pieces and possible moves. In 2016, world champion Lee Sedol was beaten by an AI called **ALPHAGO**.

In 2018, a robot broke the world record for solving a Rubik's cube. It did it in 0.38 seconds. The best human "speed-cubers" do it in around four to five seconds. I've been trying for four days . . .

In 2019, a nimble-fingered **ROBOTIC HAND** solved a **RUBIK'S CUBE**. The AI program had to learn moves that would take a human 10,000 years to complete!

41

ROBOTS LIKE US

Meet the robots that copy our moves and steal our looks!

HUMANOIDS

These robots have a **HUMAN BODY** shape, but still look like robots. Leonardo's robot knight was an early humanoid! (see page 13).

Humanoids can imitate **HUMAN MOVEMENT** and perform simple actions, but they can't move as well as humans yet.

DIGITAL VIDEO CAMERA EYES

JOINTED BODY FOR FLEXIBLE MOVEMENT

ASIMO

ICUB

Humanoid robot **ASIMO** can walk up and down stairs.

Meet **ICUB**, a kid-sized humanoid that is programmed to learn and remember—just like a real child. It can play chess and even use a bow and arrow!

ANDROIDS

These robots are designed to look and act like humans. They are built to interact with people.

Androids have realistic skin and hair.

ANDROID GEMINOID DK

HUMAN MODEL FOR GEMINOID DK

MECHANICS UNDER FAKE SKIN

Some android body parts, like faces and arms, are made from silicone casts of **ACTUAL PEOPLE**!

SOPHIA is an android that can speak, laugh, make facial expressions, and even tell jokes!

Research shows that up to a point people find humanoids cute or "goofy." However, the more lifelike robots become, the more frightening people find them. Maybe because they look human but they aren't really alive!

DID YOU HEAR THE ONE ABOUT THE INVISIBLE DROID?

IT WAS CALLED C-THROUGH-P.O.

NOT LIFELIKE

GOOFY HUMANOID

CREEPY PUPPET

SCARY ANDROID

LIFELIKE

43

ROBOTS THAT CARE

ARE YOU READY TO BE CARED FOR BY A HIGH-TECH TEDDY BEAR OR A ROBO-NURSE?

BRAINIAC HACK: SOCIAL ROBOTS

Robots don't have feelings yet, but **SOCIAL ROBOTS** have artificial intelligence that learns to recognize and react when humans interact with them.

PEPPER GREETS PATIENTS.

ROBEAR CAN HELP PATIENTS STAND UP.

Social robots can be used in **HOSPITALS** and **CARE HOMES**, working with patients as helpers, carers, and companions.

Social robots can be **HUMANOIDS**, **ANDROIDS**, or **ANIMALS**. They can understand speech, respond to touch, and recognize emotions.

CUDDLY SEAL "PARO" CALMS PEOPLE AND KEEPS THEM COMPANY.

Programming a robot to seem to care is not the same as the robot really caring. But does it matter if robots can make people feel better? How would you feel about a robot taking care of you?

PULLING FACES

Over **FORTY FACE MUSCLES** move your forehead, eyebrows, nose, mouth, and eyes to express your moods and emotions.

Programmers can train social robots to recognize emotions by showing them thousands of different faces and telling them what emotions they reveal.

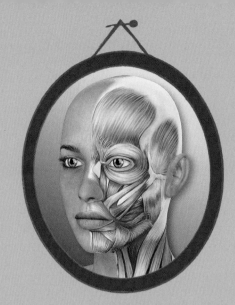

TRY THIS

FACE-OFF

Can you name the feeling shown on each of these faces?

A

B

C

D

E

F

You can find the answers on page 62.

ARTIFICIAL ART

CAN A MACHINE BE PROGRAMMED TO BE CREATIVE?

Programmers can train an AI to make art. They show it thousands of images which the AI uses to create its own pictures—but is it actually creative or is technology the real talent?

ARTWORK CREATED BY AN AI

HUMAN-MADE V. MACHINE-MADE

Humans can **EXPRESS FEELINGS** and **IDEAS** through art. What they create has a purpose and meaning.

Machines don't have feelings or ideas. However, they can **REMIX OLD IDEAS** to create something new.

I MUST CAPTURE HER SMILE . . .

Humans are **INSPIRED** by the world around them and by other people's creative work.

AIs can be "inspired" by works of art, but their **PROGRAMMERS CHOOSE** the examples they learn from.

 FLIP BACK <<< to page 38 to find out more about **ARTIFICIAL INTELLIGENCE**

This portrait created by an AI made history when it sold for $432,500 at auction. The AI was shown 15,000 portraits for inspiration!

AIs can use 3D printers to print their art. The printers lay lots of thin layers of ink, one on top of the other, to copy the bumpy brushstrokes of human-made works.

ANDROID ARTIST

The world's first robot artworks were painted by **AI-DA**, an ultra-realistic android powered by artificial intelligence.

When Ai-Da looks in a mirror, **CAMERAS** in her eyes scan her facial features. She then picks up a pen or pencil with her **ROBOTIC ARM** and draws a self-portrait onto paper.

ROBOT SHOWTIME!

DATA DUMP

Remember automata? Meet their modern-day robot relatives.
IT'S CURTAIN UP FOR THE PROGRAMMED PERFORMERS!

Our first act is a
ROBOT FLUTE PLAYER.
It uses mechanical lungs to
blow, and a mechanical tongue
and lips to toot its flute.

TOOT TOOT

HAVE YOU HEARD MY NEW ALBUM?

Please welcome on stage
singer-songwriter **SHIMON!**
This four-armed marimba player
can even jam along with its very
own human jazz band.

Shimon is the first ever
robot to have taken part in
a **RAP BATTLE**. It can react to
a real-life rapper by coming up
with lyrics on the spot.

FLIP BACK <<< to page 12 to find out more about **AUTOMATA**

Next up is robot actor and presenter **ROBOTHESPIAN**. It can be programmed to perform speeches and songs, complete with facial expressions and actions.

I NEVER FORGET MY LINES.

Let's hear it for **ATLAS**, the super-agile robot famous for its dance moves. It can leap, tumble, and do 360° spins in midair!

These robots are fun, but they have also helped to test new robot technology. Atlas is being developed to carry out search and rescue tasks.

ROAAAAR!

EEEK!

And finally, meet the frighteningly real **ANIMATRONIC DINOSAURS** that really bring museum exhibits to life. Some dinos even have motion sensors to react to visitors that get up close.

A STEEL SKELETON AND MACHINERY ARE HIDDEN UNDER REALISTIC DINO SKIN.

49

ATHLETIC ROBOTS

DIFFERENT SPORTS PUT ROBOT SKILLS TO THE TEST!

> BALL DETECTED.
> WHERE AM I?
> PASS OR SHOOT?
> WHERE IS MY GOAL?
> WHERE IS MY TEAM?

BRAINIAC HACK: ROBOT SOCCER

Robots are good at **FOLLOWING RULES**, but games like soccer help scientists find ways to get robots to work as a **TEAM**.

EVERY YEAR, ROBOT TEAMS FROM AROUND THE WORLD COMPETE IN THE ROBOT SOCCER WORLD CUP

PROGRAMMED TO PLAY

THINK:
Robot players use AI to make decisions.

COMMUNICATE:
Speakers, microphones, lights, and wi-fi let robots send and receive messages.

SENSE:
Different sensors measure distance, tell the robot its position and let it "feel" the ground and the ball.

To ever beat a human team one day, robots need to be faster at **MOVING**, **REACTING**, and **PREDICTING** what will happen next.

FLIP BACK <<< to page 20 to find out more about **ROBOT SENSORS**

ONE-ON-ONE

In **ROBOT-SUMO** two **SUMOBOTS** try to push each other out of a ring, just like real sumo wrestlers. They use sensors to find their opponent.

SMASH!

PING-PONG ROBOTS don't need legs to run around. They use long, robotic arms to return the ball. **FORPHEUS** can react so fast it plays humans—and wins!

TRY THIS

SOLO SKILLS

Robots can be programmed to copy some human movements.

Basketball robot **CUE3** can shoot over 2,000 hoops without a miss!

Try tossing scrunched-up paper balls into a trash can from five steps away. How many can you score without a miss?

EXPLANATION:

Robots can repeat the same action without getting tired or distracted. For humans, perfect aim takes coordination, concentration, and dedication!

ROBOTS ON THE ROAD

Get ready to be transported into the future—robot cars are just round the corner!

NEED-TO-KNOW FACTS

Scientists and engineers are developing self-driving, or **AUTONOMOUS, CARS**. Here's how they work:

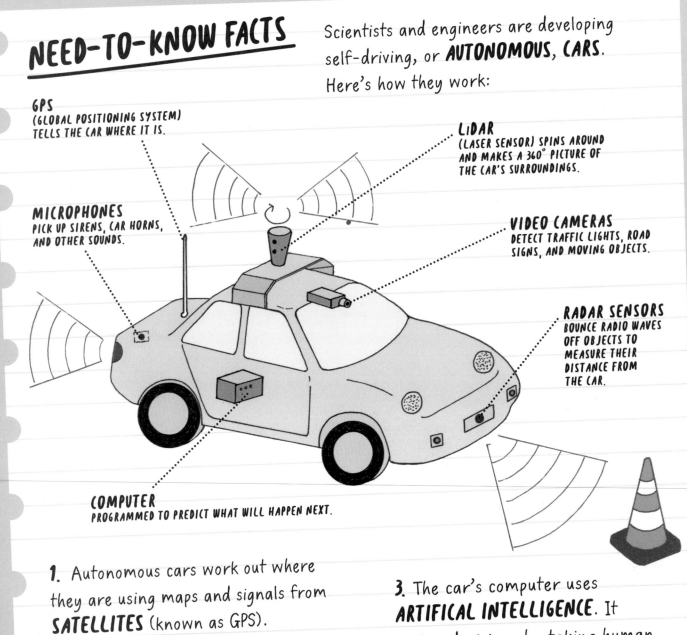

GPS
(GLOBAL POSITIONING SYSTEM)
TELLS THE CAR WHERE IT IS.

LiDAR
(LASER SENSOR) SPINS AROUND
AND MAKES A 360° PICTURE OF
THE CAR'S SURROUNDINGS.

MICROPHONES
PICK UP SIRENS, CAR HORNS,
AND OTHER SOUNDS.

VIDEO CAMERAS
DETECT TRAFFIC LIGHTS, ROAD
SIGNS, AND MOVING OBJECTS.

RADAR SENSORS
BOUNCE RADIO WAVES
OFF OBJECTS TO
MEASURE THEIR
DISTANCE FROM
THE CAR.

COMPUTER
PROGRAMMED TO PREDICT WHAT WILL HAPPEN NEXT.

1. Autonomous cars work out where they are using maps and signals from **SATELLITES** (known as GPS).

2. They use **SENSORS**, including LiDAR, radar, video cameras, and microphones to check what is around them.

3. The car's computer uses **ARTIFICAL INTELLIGENCE**. It makes decisions by taking human drivers' knowledge that it has been programmed with and information from its sensors.

Over 90% of car crashes are caused by human mistakes! More self-driving cars should lead to safer roads.

CRUNCH!

HOW DO SELF-DRIVING CARS HEAR?

THEY ARE MADE BY ENGINE-EARS!

ARE ROBOT CARS GOOD OR BAD?

✓

✗

✔ FEWER ACCIDENTS
✔ NO ROAD RAGE
✔ TRANSPORT FOR DISABLED AND ELDERLY PEOPLE
✔ SELF-PARKING CARS SAVE TIME
✔ PEOPLE CAN WORK OR REST WHILE CAR DRIVES

✗ TAXI AND DELIVERY DRIVERS WOULD LOSE WORK
✗ SENSORS DON'T WORK AS WELL IN CERTAIN WEATHER, SUCH AS SNOW
✗ PEOPLE WOULD FORGET THEIR DRIVING SKILLS

PROBLEM: if an autonomous car crashes WHO IS TO BLAME? The car's maker, the AI, or the passenger?

PHANTOM FARMERS!

Some self-driving farm vehicles are already used to plant and harvest crops. Fields are perfect for autonomous tractors because they can move slowly and there are no cars to crash into!

BEEP! BEEP!

BAAA!

BAAAA!

DATA DUMP

INTO THE FUTURE

Check out some incredible robots that are being worked on right now.
ROBOTS LOOK SET TO IMPROVE LIFE ON THIS PLANET—AND BEYOND!

ROBOBEE

BEE

Mini robots known as **SWARM BOTS** are being developed to **WORK TOGETHER** like busy bees or an army of ants. These robots may be as small as a coin, but together they could pollinate whole fields of crops.

NANOBOT

RED BLOOD CELL

One day, doctors may be able to inject microscopic robots, called **NANOBOTS**, into patients. Smaller than a red blood cell, they could **BATTLE BACTERIA**, viruses or cancer cells inside the body.

NASA's **VALKYRIE** is a tough humanoid space robot being developed for a **MISSION TO MARS.** It could set up camp before human astronauts arrive.

ROBOT EXOSKELETONS are already used to boost human strength and help people with mobility problems walk. In the future, maybe we'll all be wearing them when we need to save energy.

IT FEELS LIGHT AS A FEATHER!

THUMB, PRESS "SEND."

Missing arms and legs can be replaced by **ROBOTIC LIMBS**. In the future, their movements will be completely controlled by the person's mind.

Will robo-pets scamper alongside our fluffy friends in the future? Come on Sci-Fido, time for cyber-walkies!

GUESS WHAT?
A HUMAN THAT UPGRADES THEIR BODY WITH ROBOT PARTS IS CALLED A CYBORG (CYBERNETIC ORGANISM).

A WORLD RULED BY ROBOTS?

One day, robots with artificial intelligence may become smarter than humans. This situation is called the **TECHNOLOGICAL SINGULARITY** and it could cause problems . . .

BOSSY ROBOTS

Some experts worry that AI will develop beyond our control and we might end up working for robots!

CONFUSED ROBOTS

Other experts think humans are the problem. Robots are programmed to follow orders, but what if a human tells a robot to do something illegal?

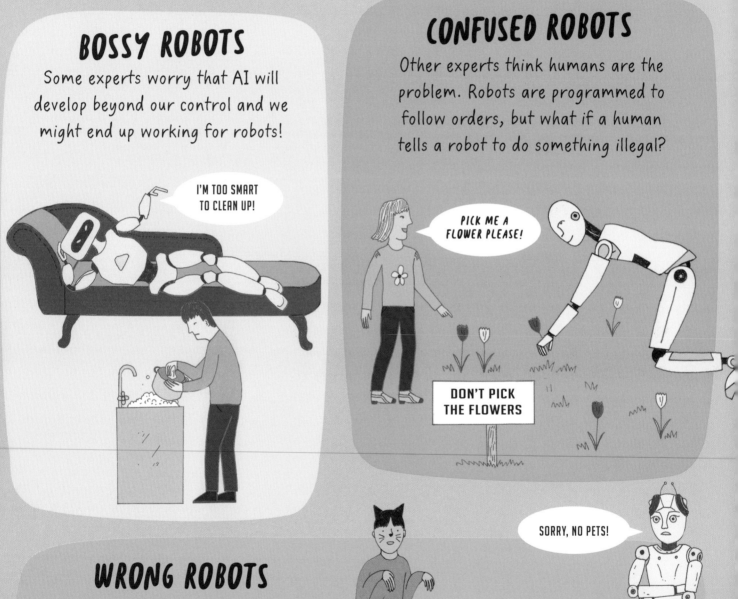

I'M TOO SMART TO CLEAN UP!

PICK ME A FLOWER PLEASE!

DON'T PICK THE FLOWERS

SORRY, NO PETS!

COSTUME PARTY

WRONG ROBOTS

Robots can be programmed to make decisions, but if the information they are given isn't balanced they may make unfair decisions!

Should thinking, feeling robots of the future have rights just like humans? Or are we robots just mechanical servants?

RIGHTS FOR ROBOTS!

RIGHTS FOR ROBOTS!

ROBOT LAWS

The science fiction writer Isaac Asimov suggested three laws for how robots and humans might live together safely:

WHAT LAWS would you program into a future robot?

LAWS OF ROBOTS

1 A ROBOT SHOULD NEVER HURT A HUMAN OR BY NOT DOING ANYTHING ALLOW A HUMAN TO GET HURT.

2 A ROBOT MUST OBEY HUMANS (UNLESS IT GOES AGAINST LAW 1)

3 A ROBOT MUST PROTECT ITSELF (UNLESS IT GOES AGAINST LAWS 1 AND 2)

MY ROBOT LAWS

1 STAY OUT OF MY ROOM

2 NO BORROWING MY SKATEBOARD

3 DON'T TELL IF YOU DO MY HOMEWORK

4 . . .

ROBOTS: THE STORY SO FAR . . .

From wind-up toys to jaw-dropping droids, meet the robots that have made history.

"THE MUSICIAN," c. 1774

Automata like this one were the first robots. Their wind-up workings could be arranged to make them do different things.

SHAKEY, 1966

Shakey was the first robot with built-in AI. It used a camera and bump sensors to avoid obstacles and move across a room.

ELEKTRO, 1938

As soon as electricity was used to power robots, they were able to do much more.

SPARKO THE ROBOT DOG

THWACK!

IN 1966, UNIMATE APPEARED ON TV DOING TRICKS LIKE HITTING A GOLF BALL!

Being powered by electricity meant Elektro could walk, talk, respond to voice commands, and even blow up balloons!

UNIMATE, 1961

This industrial robot worked in factories welding and stacking metal car parts with its robotic arm.

DEEP SPACE 1, 1998

The launch of this space probe marked a big leap forward for spacecraft. It had AI software that allowed it to fix problems without human help.

AIBO, 1999

Plastic puppy Aibo started a trend for robotic pets. It learns its own name, responds to commands and being patted, and plays with toys.

FIREFLY, 2015

This completely autonomous car made the first road trip. It didn't have a steering wheel or any pedals to control it.

ANDROID ROBOT SOPHIA IMITATES SIXTY HUMAN FACIAL EXPRESSIONS.

DIGIT, 2019

This robot can go anywhere humans go. Digit will work in warehouses, lifting and carrying. In the future it could even deliver packages to your door!

SOPHIA, 2016

Sophia was the first android robot to look and behave like a real person.

GLOSSARY

3D PRINTER
A 3D printer can "print" solid objects by building up layers of plastic or other materials.

ACTUATOR
Actuators are mechanical devices that get robots moving. One example is an electric motor turning a wheel.

ALGORITHM
An algorithm is a list of instructions that breaks a job down into a series of steps.

ANDROID
An android is a robot that has been built to look, move, and interact with people like a human being.

ARTIFICIAL INTELLIGENCE (AI)
Computer programming that allows machines to do jobs that require any form of intelligence.

ARTIFICIAL NEURAL NETWORK
A type of AI that processes information in a similar way to the cells in a human brain.

AUTOMATON
An automaton is a mechanical model that imitates the movements of a person or an animal. Automata don't sense or react to their surroundings like robots.

AUTONOMOUS CAR
Also known as driverless cars, these robotic vehicles are being developed to drive themselves.

BINARY
A number system that uses just the digits 0 and 1 to encode information so that computers can process it.

BIOMIMICRY
Robot engineers are sometimes inspired by nature and copy animal body parts and how they move. This is called biomimicry.

CODE
A language that programmers use to give computers instructions. Programs in code tell robots what to do and how to do it.

COMPUTER PROGRAM
A list of instructions that a computer follows in order to process information and do jobs. A set of computer programs is called software.

DIGITAL

Any device that works with information that has been turned into 0s and 1s (binary) is digital.

DRONE

A type of flying robot that can be controlled by humans or completely automated. Drones are usually used to observe events on the ground.

EXPERT SYSTEM

A type of artificial intelligence that stores knowledge from human experts. It uses this information to make decisions.

GENERAL ARTIFICIAL INTELLIGENCE

Most artificial intelligence programs are only successful with limited and specialized tasks. A general AI would be able to think as flexibly as a human.

GPS (GLOBAL POSITIONING SYSTEM)

A network of GPS satellites in space send out signals that can be used with digital maps to determine where you are.

HUMANOID

A robot that has a human body shape and walks on two legs, but still looks like a robot.

INDUSTRIAL ROBOT

Industrial robots are designed to work in factories doing jobs such as heavy lifting or repetitive tasks such as assembling products.

NANOBOT

A type of microscopically small robot being developed that may be used for jobs such as carrying out repairs inside the human body.

REMOTE CONTROL

Some robots are worked from a distance by human operators using remote control (RC).

SENSORS

Devices that give robots information about where they are and the world around them. They are the robot equivalent of human senses.

SOCIAL ROBOTS

Social robots have AIs that recognize and respond to human interaction. They work with people and can do caregiving jobs.

TECHNOLOGICAL SINGULARITY

In the future robots with artificial intelligence may become smarter than their human creators. That situation is called the technological singularity.

ULTRAVIOLET LIGHT

A powerful type of radiation related to visible light that is harmful to living things and can be used to kill germs.

WE WANT ANSWERS!

10   SPOT THE BOT!

1. A **VENDING MACHINE** does just one job and isn't very "programmable," so it is usually considered an automated machine. Verdict: "not-bot."

2. An **AUTOMATED BARRIER** does have sensors and may resemble a robot arm, but it does just one job and can't be programmed to do anything else. Verdict: "not-bot."

3. A **WASHING MACHINE** can be programmed to wash clothes, but nothing else. "Programming" it is not much different from setting an alarm clock. Verdict: "not-bot."

4. Some **DRONES** make their own decisions and so are more robot-like, while others are more like remote control toys. Verdict: robots and "not-bots."

5. A **ROBOTIC LAWN MOWER** does just one job and works in a very specific place. It's not that smart, but it does makes some decisions. Verdict: robot.

6. DRIVERLESS CARS currently still need to have a human ready to take the steering wheel, but they do make decisions. Verdict: robot.

7. This **REMOTE-CONTROLLED BOAT** is operated by humans and doesn't do much but move around. Verdict: "not-bot."

8. COMPUTERS are the "brains" for many real robots, but they aren't robots themselves because they don't have a body and are stuck in one place. Verdict: "not-bots."

9. A **SMART SPEAKER** or digital assistant acts as if it understands you, but its responses are automated. Besides, it doesn't have a body. Verdict: "not-bot."

10. Known as a **MEDICAL CARE ROBOT**—the clue is in the name. Verdict: robot. (Did you find it easier to label this because it looked more human, like a movie robot?)

16   MECHANICAL MOVERS

The ostrich inspired the two-legged robot.
The fish inspired the underwater wildlife spy.
The insect inspired the hexapod robot.

27   MAZE ESCAPE

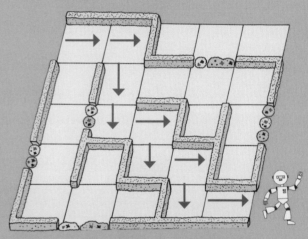

45   FACE-OFF

FIND OUT MORE . . .

spaceplace.nasa.gov/space-robots
codeclubworld.org
tinybop.com/apps/the-robot-factory
stemettes.org/girls

INDEX

PAUL VIRR

lives in Rome and writes children's books on all kinds of subjects, including science and technology. As a STEM ambassador he learned a lot about science and engineering from children, who always asked very smart (and difficult) questions at science workshops.

HARRIET RUSSELL

is the illustrator of over ten books for children including *The Brainiac's Book of the Climate and Weather* and the bestselling *This Book Thinks You're a Scientist*, published by Thames & Hudson. She lives in London.

DR. JAMES LLOYD

is a science communicator and journalist who is currently Science Writer at The Alan Turing Institute—the UK's national institute for AI and data science.

The Brainiac's Book of Robots and AI © 2023 Thames & Hudson Ltd, London
Text © 2023 Paul Virr
Illustrations © 2023 Harriet Russell

Edited by Cath Ard
Designed by Belinda Webster
Scientific consultant Dr. James Lloyd

First published in the United States of America in 2023 by
Thames & Hudson Inc., 500 Fifth Avenue, New York, New York 10110

Library of Congress Control Number 2022945755

ISBN 978-0-500-65286-2

Printed in China by RR Donnelley

MIX
Paper from responsible sources
FSC® C144853

Be the first to know about our new releases, exclusive content and author events by visiting
thamesandhudson.com
thamesandhudsonusa.com
thamesandhudson.com.au

Photography credits
a = above; b = below; c = centre; l = left; r = right

page 10a: noina/Shutterstock
page 10bl: UlfsFotoart/Shutterstock
page 10bc: Gorodenkoff/Shutterstock
page 10br: Iurii Osadchi/Shutterstock
page 11al: Tuttoo/Shutterstock
page 11ac: ChiccoDodiFC/Shutterstock
page 11ar: Aerial-motion/Shutterstock
page 11bl: Gorodenkoff/Shutterstock
page 11bc: Proxima Studio/Shutterstock
page 11br: Miriam Doerr Martin Frommherz/Shutterstock
page 20ar: Pixel Enforcer/Alamy
page 20l: 25krunya/Shutterstock
page 20c: Audrius Merfeldas/Shutterstock
page 20bl: Photo Kate Haynes
page 20br: pdsci/Shutterstock
page 21c: Maximillian Cabinet/Shutterstock
page 24ar: GL Archive/Alamy
page 24bl: GL Archive/Alamy
page 24br: GRANGER - Historical Picture Archive/Alamy
page 25al: Anonymous, *Portrait of Augusta Ada King-Noel, Countess of Lovelace*, 1840. IanDagnall Computing/Alamy
page 25bl: Pictorial Press Ltd/Alamy
page 39b: Science History Images/Alamy
page 42ar: catwalker/Shutterstock
page 42bl: Antonello Marangi/Shutterstock
page 43a: REUTERS/Juan Carlos Ulate/Alamy
page 43b: Anton Gvozdikov/Shutterstock
page 44ar: BSIP SA/Alamy
page 44l: Newscom/Alamy
page 44br: ROBOT-SEAL/ REUTERS/Kim Kyung-Hoon/Alamy
page 45a: Derya Cakirsoy/Shutterstock
page 46a: Oxia Palus in the style of Gustav Klimt and Vincent van Gogh, *No.5 - The Night Kiss - Origins II*, 2021. Oxia Palus (2021)
page 46l, 46cl: Leonardo da Vinci, *Mona Lisa*, 1503. Musée du Louvre, Paris
page 46cr: Katsushika Hokusai, *The Great Wave*, 1830-33. Art Institute Chicago. Clarence Buckingham Collection
page 46r: Vincent van Gogh, *Sunflowers*, 1889. Oil on canvas, Philadelphia Museum of Art. The Mr. and Mrs. Carroll S. Tyson, Jr., Collection, 1963
page 47a: Obvious, *Portrait of Edmond de Belamy*, 2018. Obvious - @obvious-art
page 47bl: Ai-Da Robot, *Ai-Da Robot paints Queen Elizabeth II - making history as the first humanoid robot to paint Royalty*, 2022. Copyright © Aidan Meller www.ai-darobot.com
page 47br: Ai-Da Robot, *Ai-Da Robot looks into a mirror to create a self portrait - what does it mean to be a "self"*, 2022. Copyright © Aidan Meller www.ai-darobot.com
page 50: Imaginechina Limited/Alamy
page 51b: Aflo Co. Ltd./Alamy
page 53b: Scharfsinn/Alamy
page 54: World History Archive/Alamy
page 55ar: Gorodenkoff/Shutterstock
page 55l: UfaBizPhoto/Shutterstock
page 58c: Science History Images/Alamy
page 59a: John Muggenborg/Alamy
page 59b: Anton Gvozdikov/Shutterstock